LUKE'S WAY

JOHN LUCAS

with Jeanne Engelmann

■ HAZELDEN®

Hazelden Educational Materials
Center City, Minnesota 55012-0176

ISBN: 1-56838-029-1

Editor's note

Hazelden Educational Materials offers a variety of information on lifelong recovery from chemical dependency and other addictions. Our publications do not necessarily represent Hazelden's rehabilitation programs, nor do they officially speak for any Twelve Step organization.

Cover photographs courtesy of Nathaniel S. Butler, Andrew D. Bernstein, and Charles Cyr

Inside photographs courtesy of the following:
Martha Easterling: p. 2
The collection of John and Blondola Lucas: Nat Purefoy, p.5; Harold Moore, p. 10;
Hillside High School Yearbook 1972, p. 13; Joel Golden, p. 16
The archives of the NBA: Houston Rockets, p. 21; Golden State Warriors, p. 24;
Andrew D. Bernstein, p. 36; Tim Defresco, p. 40; Nathaniel S. Butler, p. 44

Lucas, John (John H.)
    Luke's Way / John Lucas with Jeanne Engelmann.
    p.   cm.
    ISBN 1-56838-029-1
    1. Lucas, John (John H.) --Juvenile literature. 2. Basketball
players--United States--Biography--Juvenile literature.
3. Athletes--Drug use--United States--Case studies--Juvenile
literature. [1. Lucas, John (John H.) 2. Basketball players.
3. Afro-Americans--Biography. 4. Athletes--Drug use. 5. Drug
abuse.] I. Engelmann, Jeanne. II. Title.
GV884.L83A3 1994b
796.323'092--dc20
[B]
                                                                    94-29592
                                                                        CIP
                                                                         AC

TABLE OF CONTENTS

ABOUT THE AUTHORS

John Lucas is head coach of the Philadelphia 76ers. A former professional basketball player and recovering drug addict, Lucas also works with drug treatment, education, and prevention programs.

Jeanne Engelmann is a freelance writer from St. Paul, Minnesota. She is the author of several Hazelden works for children and young people, including *My Body Is My House, Rule of the Szäk King,* and *Wonder What I Feel Today?*

INTRODUCTION

John Lucas, known to his friends as Luke, is a tough competitor. Now coach of the Philadelphia 76ers, John was a point guard in the NBA for fourteen years. He also played pro tennis. John showed amazing athletic talent early in life. "I played to win," he said. "Everything I did was about winning. I wanted to do everything perfectly."

Throughout his school years, John excelled in basketball and tennis. At seventeen, he played tennis on the United States Junior Davis Cup team. At twenty-two, he was the first pick in the 1976 NBA draft. He had money and fame, so what was next?

After three years in the NBA, John found that he was addicted to alcohol and cocaine. The disease of addiction began affecting his play, and he missed practices and games. John was on a downward spiral that lasted several years. He tried treatment but it didn't work. One morning John woke up in downtown Houston. He had blacked out—he remembered nothing from the night before. He wore a suit but had no shoes. He wore shades, hoping no one would recognize him. John had hit bottom.

He went into treatment for chemical dependency, and this time it worked. He sobered up and changed everything about his life in order to stay sober.

Good things are happening for John now—only because he works hard every day to stay off alcohol and other drugs. Being honest with himself and helping others help John stay sober. What did Luke learn? Be the best you can be, but leave the obsession to win on the court. There's a lot more to life than winning games, and you need to develop all sides of yourself as you grow up.

John with Coach Carl Easterling

Chapter One
BORN TO WIN

I started my basketball career shooting aluminum foil balls into wastebaskets with my sister, Cheryl. When we were kids, we'd run around the house guarding each other as we made fancy shots at the baskets.

My family lived in Durham, North Carolina. My mother was an assistant principal in a middle school, and my father was the principal of Hillside High School, the largest black high school in the state. When I was in elementary school, I'd walk to Hillside after my classes were done, to wait until my father was done for the day. I loved to hang around the gym and watch the athletes. The high school coach, Carl Easterling, taught me both basketball and tennis. He was my first important role model outside my family.

I hung out around the tennis courts when the high school team practiced. I chased balls for the tennis team because there were no backstops. I got the idea of stopping the balls with a racket and knocking them back to the players. That's how my interest in tennis really began.

When I was ten, Coach Easterling started teaching me tennis. I won the first tennis tournament I played in and kept on winning. I was always very competitive. Sometimes my competitive nature got me in trouble. I remember a time in fifth grade when I played in a baseball game, boys against the girls. The girls were cheating—at least we boys thought so. But my teacher wouldn't put a stop to it. I got so furious with her that she wouldn't let me play the next day.

My parents made sure I took enough time to study. I did well in school but didn't find it as exciting as sports. Textbooks laid everything out for you. I preferred to find new ways of solving problems and learning. I loved the challenge of facing something new. And in tennis, each match was different. I liked the challenge of never knowing how the next point would play.

From third grade on I was always playing in tournaments or attending sports camps. I never really spent summer like most kids do—never climbed a tree or went fishing. I still don't know how to swim. I didn't spend much time with kids outside of school, except around sports. Instead of friends, I had teammates.

John on his way to the North Carolina
State Men's Tennis Championship

Chapter Two
FOURTEEN-YEAR-OLD CHAMP

By the time I was in seventh grade, I played basketball well enough to start on the junior high varsity team. I led the city in scoring. We won fifteen games in a row during my ninth grade year.

As a tenth grader, I was good enough to play varsity basketball. But the school had a rule that students had to play on the junior varsity team for their first year. My dad didn't want to change the rule, because he didn't want the principal's kid to be the exception. He left it up to the coaches and players to vote. They agreed to let me start on the varsity team when a place opened up later in the season.

At the same time, I was also improving my tennis. I played in many tournaments in North Carolina and nearby states. Either my father or Coach Easterling went with me on these trips. The trips were expensive. But I was fortunate to grow up in a close, supportive African-American neighborhood. The community gave money to help me travel to these tournaments.

My tournament play gave me the confidence I needed to enter the Durham City-County Tennis Championship in 1968. I was fourteen at the time. I signed up for every event I was eligible for—fourteen and under singles and doubles, sixteen and under singles and doubles, eighteen and under singles and doubles, and men's singles and doubles. I won seven of these events, including men's singles, and my photo was in the "Faces in the Crowd" section of *Sports Illustrated*.

Because desegregation was just beginning in the South, I was often the only African American playing in tennis tournaments. And at tennis camps I was a loner because of the racism. In a tennis tournament in Chattanooga, Tennessee, the referees kept calling me for foot faults (stepping on the baseline while serving). There was no way I was faulting that much, but what could I do? I ended up losing. I also remember not being allowed to use the locker room and toilet facilities at a tournament because of my race.

I reacted to these barriers by playing my best and never showing any emotion on the court. That carried over into the rest of my life, because I learned to keep everything inside.

My success in tennis tournament play helped me advance to play in tournaments sponsored by the American Tennis

Association (ATA), a black tennis organization. I was fourteen, but I didn't play in the fourteen and under events. It wasn't a challenge anymore. I played in men's events—and won. I won two ATA titles. That helped prepare me for the United States Lawn Tennis Association (USLTA), a major circuit for tennis.

I also played in the North Carolina State Men's Tennis Tournament two years in a row—when I was fourteen and fifteen years old. I lost both times to the same guy for the championship. He was was in his twenties. It was exciting to play against someone so much more experienced than me. The big crowd was also exciting. After playing in front of thousands of people at tennis tournaments, I was comfortable in front of the crowds at high school basketball games. When the other guys would get nervous I'd say, "What's the matter? There's nobody out there!"

I was developing unrealistic goals. In my world, seventh graders played varsity basketball; fourteen-year-olds won adult tennis tournaments. It never occurred to me that I might not be good enough. In high school I won 186 tennis matches and lost 28. I had a string of 31 consecutive matches without a loss and was seeded first in the 1972 USLTA championships. Coach Easterling said I was the greatest natural athlete he'd ever seen.

I always wanted to stand out from the crowd. I dreamed

about being different—a little flashier, a little more trendy. I was known for a couple of quirks in high school. Players were required to bring two cans of balls to high school tennis tournaments. The loser of each match was supposed to give the extra can to the winner. I took just one can. To bring any more would be to admit I might lose. I also refused to change out of my warm-ups.

To me, winning wasn't everything—it was the *only* thing. That meant there was no such thing as compromise in my life. I either won or I lost—there was nothing in between. I focused narrowly on my two favorite sports and the success I found there. I thought beating adults meant I *was* an adult. I grew as an athlete, but not as a *person*.

John was a high school All-American in basketball as well as tennis.

Chapter Three
COURTING DREAMS

As I got older, my tennis got better and better. Some people called me the next Arthur Ashe. Ashe heard about my playing and came to meet me. We stayed in touch for years. He used to send me his tennis rackets.

I won a place on the U. S. Junior Davis Cup team when I was seventeen. It was the highlight of my high school tennis career. I was the first African American ever to be named to the squad. I competed with top players like Jimmy Connors and Vitas Gerulaitis. Over three hundred colleges wanted to give me tennis scholarships.

I continued to excel in basketball as well. I averaged thirty-five points a game in my senior year in high school. I led my team to the North Carolina state basketball tournament. I was a two-sport All-American in high school.

During these years, my parents felt my job was to do my best in sports. I didn't have chores to do. My father was afraid

I might cut my hands if I did dishes, so I led a special life. As I got older, I found that athletes continue to get special treatment. People helped make life both inside and outside of sports easier. That special treatment led me to believe that someone would always be there to help me.

I did well in school. I had almost total recall and rarely forgot anything. If I was challenged in my studies, I was able to be one of the best in school. Other times, I turned my class work into a game and tried to find a different way to do it. I especially enjoyed class debates and making presentations.

I first tried alcohol when I was fifteen. I had heard other kids talk about wine and beer, but I didn't know what to expect. I didn't like the taste, so I was surprised at alcohol's powerful effect on me. The high from alcohol made it seem easier to be part of the group, not separate from other kids. Alcohol also made me feel better because it eased the pressure I felt to be the best.

Alcohol gave me a false feeling of wholeness like what I felt when playing tennis or basketball. But I didn't drink very much in high school. I drank as part of a social activity. I was too involved with sports to hang around with the kids who drank at the local hangout.

Sometimes alcohol also seemed to help me deal with dating. If I'd been drinking, I didn't feel hurt if I got rejected. I dated

John's high school classmate and sweetheart, Debbie Fozard

different girls, but there was one girl I was especially interested in. We lived four blocks apart and had known each other since elementary school. Her name was Debbie Fozard.

Debbie remembers me as a joker. When I'd pass by the classroom door and see her, I'd stop to do something silly to make her laugh. I told Debbie all through junior high that I was going to marry her. I'd tease her and say things like, "I'm going to marry you, girl." She'd say, "I wouldn't marry you if you were the last person on Earth." She thought I was too full of myself. In our senior year I was still teasing her, and she finally started talking to me. She said she'd always liked me. We went to different colleges, but we kept in touch until we got back together and then married in 1979.

My yearbook says my ambition is to be "the first black president of the U. S." What a goal! I wanted to go right to the top. I wanted to be the best professional tennis and basketball player. And my "field of dreams" was becoming a reality.

Chapter Four
TIME TO CHOOSE: TENNIS OR BASKETBALL?

Graduation from high school was a hard but exciting time for me. I hated the idea of all the changes ahead. But I also had offers from colleges all over the country in two sports. Before I could make a college decision, I had to choose between my two best sports: Would I choose tennis or basketball?

Several things helped me make my decision. Arthur Ashe wrote me a letter with some suggestions about choosing between tennis and basketball. I had to weigh how I felt about playing alone (tennis) or playing as part of a team (basketball).

I thought a lot about how I felt about each sport. While I knew I was a better tennis player, I decided I just didn't like the loneliness it involved. You traveled by yourself and never got to know any of the other players because they were from all over the country. I liked the camaraderie of basketball—the team experience.

I finally chose basketball and the University of Maryland. I liked the coach, Lefty Driesell. I asked him, "Coach, if I'm good enough to start, will you play me?" He said, "Son, if you're the best player, you'll start." Starting was very important to me.

I also needed the structure that my close family, school, and community had provided for me throughout my life. Going to a college close to home meant I'd be able to keep some of that structure around me during college. The college was close to Washington, D.C., where I lived with my sister Cheryl. She had a lot of influence over me. My parents came up for games once or twice a week and often visited us on weekends.

Coach Driesell had some important advice for me early on. I was proud that I had scored forty and fifty points during some freshman scrimmages. But Coach Driesell said we wouldn't have a very good team if one person averaged that many points. He told me that scoring lots of points didn't necessarily win games; I had to get the ball to other people, which I started to do. He called me "coachable" because I'd listen to him and do what he told me. Driesell made me a starter my freshman year.

John directs the offense as a freshman point guard at the University of Maryland.

Chapter Five
LEADER ON THE COURT:
THE MAKING OF A GREAT POINT GUARD

My first year playing varsity basketball for the University of Maryland was great. Every home game was televised. We were very good. My teammates included Tom McMillen, Lenny Elmore, and Mo Howard.

I also played tennis for Maryland. But I hadn't taken a tennis scholarship, so the tennis team didn't even know I was coming. The tennis coach, Doyle Royal, didn't know how good I was. But after I beat everyone on the team, Coach Royal let me play number-one singles on the team that first year.

During my second year at college, I played more tennis than usual, even during the basketball season. As a result, I won the Atlantic Coast Conference (ACC) singles title my sophomore and senior years, and the doubles title my freshman and senior years.

I saw a lot more drug use on campus than I'd seen in high

school, but drugs still didn't mean much to me. I wouldn't smoke marijuana because all the people who used it got wasted. When I spotted teammates using marijuana, I'd try to mess up their high. I'd tell them they were hurting the team. In my senior year, though, I tried cocaine for the first time. And I tried it again just before graduation. I liked it, but I didn't start using it a lot yet.

During my junior year, the New Jersey Nets made me their number-one draft pick. I seriously considered taking their offer. I was upset because Coach Driesell moved me from point guard to small forward on the college team. I didn't like the idea because Mo Howard and I played well together in the backcourt. Reporters had called us the best backcourt in the country. And people kept telling me, "You'll lose your value if you play small forward."

So I was tempted by the idea of going pro a year early. I called my parents to try the idea out on them. My dad told me to think about it and pray on it. But later that night my mother called and said, "There's only one thing you ever promised me you'd do and that was to get your degree. I love you. See you later." That's all she said. So to me there was no longer a choice. I stayed in school and got my degree in business. Later I went on to get a master's degree in education as well.

I wasn't an outstanding student in college, but I wanted to

get good grades. My sister, Cheryl, reminded me that although basketball was important, the real reason I was there was to get an education. She kept me focused on school and helped me remember I was an African American. There were a lot of black athletes who forgot their heritage once they got into big white colleges. Cheryl always tried to give me a sense of my self-worth and importance. I maintained a 3.0 grade point average in my major in college.

My college graduation felt like my high school graduation—uncomfortable. I thought, Here it comes, another big change. It was another bitter time, a kind of dying for me. I didn't know what the future held, and I held the present and past very dear.

But the NBA draft was coming up, and the future promised to be exciting. I was considered the best point guard in college basketball and was expected to be drafted number one.

Chapter Six
LUCAS: NUMBER-ONE NBA DRAFT PICK

Two days before the draft, my agent called and said, "John, you need to get your suit, get on a plane, and meet me in Houston first thing in the morning." It didn't surprise me. I just told my parents and flew down to Houston.

Tom Nissalke became head coach of the Houston Rockets the year I was ready to go pro. He had identified me, Quinn Buckner of Indiana, Armond Hill of Princeton, and Ronnie Lee of Oregon State as the best point guards in college basketball. And I was at the top of his rating list. The Rockets traded another draft pick and center for the right to draft number one, and they picked me. I signed with the Houston Rockets for over a million dollars in a five-year contract.

My dreams were becoming reality. But I was running out of challenges in the sports arena. I was becoming a one-dimensional being. Basketball and tennis was becoming *who I was* rather than what I did.

The first player selected in the 1976 NBA draft, John was picked by the Houston Rockets.

At age twenty-two, I was a child in an adult athlete's body. If someone asked me, "What do you do in your spare time?" I'd say, "Watch basketball." And if I was asked, "What do you do when you aren't watching basketball?" I'd say, "Oh, I'm playing tennis." And if asked, "What do you do when you don't have a tennis match?" I'd say, "Well, I'm thinking about tennis."

The day I signed my basketball contract with the Rockets, I also signed a tennis contract. The summer before my first NBA year started, I played World Team Tennis with California's Golden Gate Gators. My teammates included Frew McMillan from South Africa and Tom "the Flying Dutchman" Okker from the Netherlands.

With my first pro basketball season ahead of me, I was anxious but excited. It was exciting to play against Dr. J in the

Spectrum, Walt Frazier and Earl Monroe in the New York Garden, and Kareem in the Forum. It was exciting to be a pro, but it wasn't like college.

I quickly realized that ultimately, playing pro basketball was a job. The players didn't go out to eat after the games. We didn't get together, the wives didn't talk to each other. I was used to sold-out arenas, booster clubs, and fans showing up from town to town. This was different. Football was king in Houston, so basketball stories often fell on page three of the sports section. And the arena was rarely sold out.

The change from my college days was big. All of a sudden I had no family, no structure. For the first time I had my own apartment and was all alone. I was very lonely. We played eighty-two games a season, three to four games a week. It was exhausting, yet I had a lot of time on my hands. We practiced an hour and a half each day and then we were through until the next practice or game. So I really looked forward to the games.

I had a good first year as a pro. When I went to the Rockets that fall, I was pretty self-confident. But I had to face that for the first time in my career I wasn't a starter. I came off the bench to back up Calvin Murphy.

Once the other players saw that I liked to pass the ball and could make plays, however, they started to warm up to me.

They saw that I could make the rest of them look a little better. Finally, twenty-eight games into the season, I began to start. Then Moses Malone came to play for the Rockets. He moved into the apartment above me, and we became very good friends. Getting Malone was the final piece in making the Rockets almost an ideal team.

We had a very good season. We won the division and went to the semifinals, but we lost to Philadelphia in the sixth game. Coach Nissalke was coach of the year, and I made the All-Rookie team.

My second year with the Rockets was a little different. Because of injuries, the team began losing. I was not used to losing, and began experimenting more with drugs.

Then came a big blow. The Rockets traded me to Golden State to get Rick Barry. When Coach Nissalke got word that I had been traded, tears came to his eyes. He said that I had been just starting to get the hang of it.

I was surprised and hurt. I'd found a home with the Rockets and felt I was playing well. But I also realized that just as playing basketball was a job to me, it was also a job to the coach. In the business, players sometimes had to move on.

John joined the Golden State Warriors in 1978, after being traded for their high scorer, Rick Barry.

Chapter Seven
LUKE'S TROUBLES BEGIN

In 1978 I moved to California to join the Golden State Warriors, where I remained until 1981. There I was even further from everyone I knew and the structure I needed. Still, my first year went well. I was traded for their star player, so I took over the star role. I averaged sixteen points a game.

But some of my teammates were using drugs. Drugs were easy to get and had become a mark of being rich and famous. Also, the dangers of drug use were not as well known at that time. People didn't think that cocaine was addictive.

Soon I was using cocaine and drinking regularly. Then came a string of personal losses. One of the most influential people in my life, Coach Easterling, died. I returned to North Carolina for his funeral. A week later my grandmother died. I also received word that my mother had cancer.

The team wasn't winning, and basketball was still second to football in California. My contract was set for the next couple of years. It didn't seem as if I could grow. I had no goals, and I lost the drive to succeed.

By my third year with Golden State, I was missing practices and games. I blamed it on other people, but a friend of mine said, "You know, people say you're using cocaine." I denied it and then missed four or five games. I lost part of my pay each time I missed a game.

The media started following me more closely. Everybody thought I had a cocaine problem, but nobody was saying it. My parents were worried about me, too. When I missed games, it was national news, and they knew that wasn't like me. With twenty games left in the season, I was suspended for a game. I came back, missed another game, and was suspended for the rest of the year.

I was tired of trying to handle everything alone, so I asked Debbie and our daughter, Tarvia, to move out to California. I thought having them there might help me stop using.

Debbie didn't know I was doing drugs for a long time, because I never used drugs in front of her. But when she moved out to California, she saw a whole different side to my personality. I was a binge user. That means I didn't use every day, so I often appeared to be myself. I fooled Debbie and other people—for a while.

After being suspended, I tried to quit using drugs. Everyone said I had a drug problem; I just denied it. But I was always needing money. I was always calling my attorney for more and more money. Drugs were taking over my life, but I didn't know they were the problem. I thought California was the problem. I thought going home to North Carolina to stay with my parents would help.

But cocaine was easy to get in Durham too. I started using by myself so no one would know that the rumors about me were true. Though I tried to hide my drug use, my parents knew. They'd find my empty cocaine bags and leave them around the house to let me know that they knew I was using.

With my name in the news, my team, fans, family, and friends watched more closely. I stepped ever closer to a dangerous edge.

Chapter Eight
THE ROUGH SIDE OF THE MOUNTAIN

Just before the end of my last season with Golden State, the Cleveland Cavaliers had offered me the first $2-million-a-year contract in basketball. But after my suspension, that deal fell through. Then the New Jersey Nets offered me a contract for around $250,000, but two days before I signed with them, I received a ticket for drunk driving. The Nets backed out of the deal.

Then I was traded to the Washington Bullets. I was thrilled to be back close to home. I thought I'd finally get some structure back into my life. But I soon began missing practices and games again. I *still* didn't think alcohol or drugs were the problem. I can now see that lying and covering up were part of my addiction. I had lost all values and had no conscience. My slips back into using were just part of the disease of addiction. I now know that although it seems simple to just stop drinking or using drugs, addicts can't stop by themselves. Some people have to "hit bottom" before they can be helped. Many die before they can let other people help them.

In December 1982, a reporter from the *Washington Post,* David DuPree, contacted me to do a story on my cocaine problem. I decided to admit I had a problem. It made the front page news in the *Washington Post* and was reported all around the country. It was the first time an NBA player publicly admitted using drugs.

But the NBA had no drug policy in place at the time and no rules about players who used drugs. When the commissioner asked me about my drug problem, I told him I used to do drugs but that I didn't use anymore. When I promised I would seek help at the end of the season, he let me go back to the Bullets.

After basketball season, I went to an outpatient drug treatment program, but I didn't put any effort into it. I thought the other people there were just weak-minded—that you just had to make your mind up not to use and then not do it anymore. But the whole time, I was still drinking.

Next I went to an inpatient treatment program in Pennsylvania. But I still had a bad attitude. I saw my stay there as a vacation, and they treated me like a star because I was a pro ballplayer. I was high again just forty-eight hours after leaving treatment.

Strength and unconditional love from his family helped John through his troubled times. Pictured above (left to right) are John; his mother, Blondola; his father, John Sr.; and his sister, Cheryl.

That summer I was going to stay clean on willpower alone. I worked out and got my body into shape, but again I missed practices and was late for games. Thirty-five games into the 1982-83 season, I was suspended again. The Bullets cut me from the team.

Since I was out of basketball for the rest of the season, I tried tennis. But my comeback was slow.

That fall I had no hope of playing with the NBA. So I joined the Lancaster Lightning in the Continental Basketball Association (CBA). I played one game and then called my friend Bob Bass of the San Antonio Spurs. I begged Bob to get me out of there. Bob sent me a plane ticket to San Antonio and signed me to play the rest of the season with the Spurs. I was still drinking and using cocaine, but I didn't miss any practices or games.

The next year Houston offered me a contract for more than the Spurs wanted to pay, so I accepted. In October 1984, I returned to Houston to play with the Rockets—and got in trouble once again.

I totaled three cars within a month. My wife, Debbie, would often stay up all night. She'd look out the window hoping I'd come home. My mother once said, "Sometimes I think we all come to the rough side of the mountain where life is real and where things don't fall easily into place." I had for sure hit the rough side of the mountain.

Chapter Nine
HITTING BOTTOM:
7:00 A.M. Somewhere in Downtown Houston

When I joined the Rockets in the fall of 1984, coach Bill Fitch made one thing perfectly clear: If I messed up once, I was out. I agreed because I felt I was on the way back. I was playing on a team that had a lot of talent and could be really good. I played in the first eight games of the regular season without using any drugs.

But then I got high again and missed a flight to get to a game in Portland, Oregon. When I finally arrived in Portland, coach Fitch made me take a drug test right away. It was positive. Fitch released me on the spot. But the NBA's new drug policy had just taken effect. They now had a "three strikes and you're out" policy: Strike one, a player was suspended with pay. Strike two, he was suspended without pay. Strike three, he was banned for at least two years. Since the policy was new, this was considered my first strike.

I returned to Houston and went back into drug treatment. There I started to admit I had a drug problem. When I got out of treatment in February, I went directly to Fitch to ask for my job back. Fitch said, "We'll help you, John." Fitch let me practice with the team. I also worked out with Fitch and attended meetings to help me stay sober. I worked hard, but once again, I began to use drugs and drink.

Finally, on March 14, 1986, I went on what was to be my last binge. My wife, who was now locking me into the house at night, had left keys in a door by mistake. So I got the keys and locked my family in the house. The next morning when I woke up, I remembered nothing that had happened the night before. It was 7:00 A.M., I was somewhere in downtown Houston. I was wearing a dirty suit and tie, no shoes, and five pairs of socks. I also wore my shades—trying not to be John Lucas.

The next day I went to practice and took a drug test. Later when I came to dress for the night's game, Fitch told me to keep my street clothes on and sit on the bench. The test results were back: positive.

That night on the bench, I told the biggest lie of my life in front of over 15,000 people. The results of the drug test weren't public yet, so I told the reporters the results were negative. The next morning the Rockets released me.It was then that I went into treatment for the last time. I was tired of living the way I was. I just wanted to be free of drugs. I was finally ready to get help. The Alcoholics Anonymous textbook outlines a Twelve Step plan that helps people recover from addiction by showing them step by step how to change their lives and stop using alcohol and other drugs. I started putting these Twelve Step ideas to work in my life.

In treatment they told me I wasn't a bad person, but someone with a disease. That really helped me. I stayed in treatment for forty-five days. When I came out, I had no job but attended Twelve Step meetings regularly. I didn't know what I was going to do. I had to come up with some way to live because I really thought basketball wasn't my territory anymore.

I was soon to realize, though, that my life was about to expand well beyond the narrow world of sports I had lived in for so long.

Chapter Ten
"I HAVE TO GIVE IT AWAY TO KEEP IT"

While I was in treatment, I developed a fitness program to help myself stay in shape. It became very popular with other patients in the program, so I decided to put together a conditioning program for people in treatment. I approached hospitals in Houston with the idea of trying my fitness program with their patients.

At first people laughed at me. Here I was a notorious addict who had been clean just ninety days. Most hospitals hire only people who've been sober at least a year. Finally, I met with Joyce Bossett at Houston International Hospital, and she agreed to give my program a chance. But she had two conditions: I had to take part in an aftercare program (follow-up help after treatment), and I had to agree to drug tests.

Joyce told me she was really interested in my program, but she also told me, "You're a high risk, and if you go down, I go down. So I'm going to keep an eye on you, and you're going to

have drug tests regularly. That's the deal. Do you want to do business with me?"

I told Bossett I'd do it. I went to the hospital every day. I attended an aftercare program and taught my fitness program. Within a year, my program was in eight hospitals.

After nine months in recovery, I became president of STAND, Students Taking Action Not Drugs, a prevention program in the Houston schools. I also started offering to introduce my fitness program to basketball team training programs. I was starting to do well.

Then something hit the news that threw me into the limelight again—but, for once, not because of my own drug use. Basketball player Lenny Bias of the University of Maryland, the number-one draft pick of the Boston Celtics, died of a cocaine overdose. Drug use became a major issue because someone had died. And because I was an NBA athlete with a known drug problem and was now in recovery, I was viewed as a spokesperson. I used this new role to get across some important messages about addiction. I explained that addiction is not a moral issue, it's a disease that can be treated.

Then in the fall of 1986 the Milwaukee Bucks asked me to play basketball again. I consulted with Joyce Bossett, who had become a mentor for me, and Charlie Grantham, president of the NBA players association. They put together a network of counselors for me in every city the NBA played in. When that was in place, I knew I'd have some someone to talk to everywhere I played.

I started playing with Milwaukee in January 1987. I averaged eighteen points a game that year, the most I ever averaged in my career. I stayed sober and continued speaking out about addiction and recovery.

I got over a thousand letters that year. Some were from parents whose kids were involved with drugs. Others were from other people struggling with drug use. I was beginning to get the message out.

For the first time in a long, long time, I was enjoying life. I was doing well in basketball, running my fitness programs, staying sober, and growing as a person. I felt more balanced than I ever had before. I felt good about myself. And I knew what I was doing every day—where I was waking up, where I'd been, who I'd been with, and what I'd said. I found I hadn't had to apologize to anyone in a year.

In the fall of 1988, I was traded to Seattle. And at the end of that season, I signed on with Houston for my fourteenth year of NBA play. I had come full circle in signing again with the Rockets. Houston coach Bill Fitch had told me in 1986 that I would never, ever play for the Rockets again. I often told people that Bill Fitch saved my life by kicking me off the team. He was the first person to stop letting me get away with things. Fitch carried an article titled "Fitch Saved Lucas' Life" in his wallet.

Meanwhile I opened treatment programs to help addicted athletes. Many athletes thought, If John Lucas can get sober, I can. I wanted to be there to help. I was always an assist guy in basketball, and now I'm giving people assists in life.

In 1991 I bought the Miami Tropics, a United States Basketball Association team. I wanted to help addicted players continue to play and keep in shape while they got treatment for their alcohol or other drug problem.

Former Cleveland State coach Kevin Mackey and Lloyd Daniels were two of my first recruits for the Tropics. I appointed Kevin Mackey head coach. Mackey told me about Lloyd Daniels. I had ten spots to fill on the team each summer. Six spots went to players who had tested positive for drugs while playing in the CBA or the NBA. For the other four spots I drafted only players who were recovering or had been at risk for some time. The Tropics offered these players a chance to maintain and showcase their skills. The first year, everyone on the team, including the rookies, got jobs in the NBA.

I had learned that it was important to make a contribution. People had helped me and now I was giving it back. One of my favorite sayings is "You've got to give it away to keep it."

In his first year as head coach, John led the San Antonio Spurs to the second round of the 1993 NBA playoffs.

Chapter Eleven
MEET THE NEW HEAD COACH

I've always watched coaches and I've always had a desire to lead. So when I started looking for something to keep me around the game I loved so much, I mentioned my interest in coaching to Bob Bass, president of the San Antonio Spurs. I said to Bob, "The next time you're ready to hire a coach, please give me a chance to interview." I left it at that. This was in 1992.

At Thanksgiving that year, Red McCombs, owner of the San Antonio Spurs, told Bass to be on the lookout for a new coach. Bass called me to find out how I felt about the idea of coaching. I was excited. Then Bob told Red, "I know you're going to think I'm crazy, but I tell you, John Lucas might be a great coach for our team." Red replied, "You know what? I believe you've got something." Two weeks later Red said to Bob, "You need to get ahold of Luke. See if he can coach our team."

That night I flew to Dallas where the Spurs were playing.

After the game, Bob and Red introduced me to the team as the new head coach. The players nearly fell off their chairs. The rest of the NBA was shocked too. I was thirty-nine years old—really young for an NBA coach—and I had never even been assistant coach. And here they gave me one of the best teams in the league.

My first coaching experience was successful. I seemed to fit well with the team. My enthusiasm and competitiveness helped the team take off. We won eighteen games in a row. The Spurs played well until the All-Star break. Then we hit a slow streak. We got into the playoffs and played well, but we lost in the second round to Phoenix. The Spurs ended the season winning forty-nine games and losing only thirty-three. That was one of the top win-loss records in the league.

My 1993-94 season was better yet: fifty-five wins and just twenty-seven losses. We made the playoffs again, but we lost to the Utah Jazz in the first round. Again we had slowed down at the end of the season. We weren't playing well as a team and couldn't get our momentum back. Still, it had been a great year.

I hated to leave the Spurs at the end of the 1993-94 season. They are a great team, and my relationship with the players was very rewarding. Unfortunately, I didn't feel support from the top management, especially after they let my friends Bob Bass and Bob Coleman go. I felt I needed to move on too.

I'm excited about being coach for the Philadelphia 76ers. Because I am also general manager and vice president of basketball operations, I have a lot more say in how to run the team.

I keep my players in good condition. When I was with the Spurs I wanted the players to feel like it was *their* team. I let them contribute. I had the final say on everything, but I also gave them a part in making decisions. I told the assistant coaches when I first took over the Spurs that the players come first. I believe in the power of players. My unique coaching style comes, in part, from what I've learned in recovery about not trying to be perfect and not controlling the people around you. I think my players know as much basketball as I do, so I need to listen.

I let my players huddle by themselves during games. I pick a player to coach the huddle and call plays. I also allow team members to set fines for players who miss practices or games. Giving the players a voice makes them give more; they want to win for themselves. Dale Ellis put it this way: "We were a team. We were winning and it wasn't just one guy. We all had a say and so we felt like we were a part of something."

I made George "Iceman" Gervin, one of the all time great Spurs, my chemistry coach. George has great people skills—he can talk to the players and get them to understand the coaching calls. George has called me a coach of the nineties because I can relate to the guys. I talk their language, which helps me get the best out of them. That's what helped me with David Robinson.

I think of myself as a father, brother, and coach to my players. I try to treat the players with that kind of affection and concern. David Robinson liked it that I worked hard and would get out there and run with the players. Dennis Rodman liked it that I got excited about the game and really got into it like he did. He told one reporter, "John is exuberant—and I'm hoping that he won't lose that."

Coach Lucas huddles with his team during a time out in 1993.

Chapter Twelve
LUKE'S HILL

Because conditioning can help all players, whether they're recovering from addiction or not, the Spurs built an artificial hill they call "Luke's Hill." Some have compared it to a mountain. Pro basketball, baseball, and football teams now use Luke's Hill to keep players in shape. To me, Luke's Hill stands for my struggle up what my mother called the "rough side of the mountain"—and my recovery. I used what I learned struggling up that mountain to recover from addiction and to help others recover, too.

I help myself by helping others. Through coaching, helping addicted players get into treatment, giving talks, and being there when people need me, I'm happy and contributing to my own recovery.

I probably could have been one of the best point guards ever to play in this league, but my drug problem stopped that. What seemed like failure, however, became a way for me to succeed.

I don't dwell on what might have been. Instead, I'm happy to be just who I am today. My addiction taught me a lot about myself. As a young kid I wasn't happy with me, but now I am. That's a gift.

Addiction can happen to anybody. I once thought an alcoholic or drug addict was a guy who lived on the park bench. I didn't know that I could be an addict or alcoholic. I thought if you could afford to buy your drugs, you didn't have a drug problem. My mom said, "John, Dad and I came to the conclusion that hundreds of other children from all walks of life have problems, so why should our child be exempt? Why couldn't it happen to John as well as someone else?"

Recovery has helped me develop a different attitude about life and competition. I tell my kids that everybody makes mistakes. Our children are active in sports. Our daughter, Tarvia, is an excellent figure skater. She's very competitive, although she doesn't push herself like her coach thinks she should. But when it comes to time to compete and perform, Tarvia's right there. John Jr. is also very competitive. No matter how big you are, he'll go up against you. Jai, my youngest son, competes with his brother the same way.

Tarvia maintains good grades even with a hectic schedule. She practices her skating three hours a day, five days a week. She plays basketball and volleyball for fun, but she says, "I put my best foot forward in ice skating. I plan on going to the 1998 Olympics—that's my goal." Tarvia enjoys competition but listens to my advice about winning. I tell her to put forth your best effort and when you do well, then you can be proud.

John Jr. plays basketball, tennis, and hockey, but he's learned that school comes first. He seems to have winning in perspective. He says, "If we win, we win, and if we don't, we don't. You can't win everything. Dad taught me that if you lose, keep your head. The most important thing about sports is that you play."

I stress to parents to tell the kids when to cut the competition off. As soon as the game ends, stop. Recovery taught me how to stop competing once the game ends. And I learned to recognize when something was good enough, rather than perfect. I'm not on a mission to get everyone off drugs. I just want to show what the gift of staying clean can do. Now I have other things outside of basketball that make me feel whole. So when the game ends, I have a life to share with others.

JOHN LUCAS: HIGHLIGHTS

1953 Born in Oxford, North Carolina.

1968 Wins seven events, including men's singles, in the Durham City-County Tennis Championship.

1971 Becomes the first African American to make the U. S. Junior Davis Cup tennis team.

1972 Enters the University of Maryland and starts as point guard on the basketball team.

1976 Chosen by the Houston Rockets as the number-one NBA draft pick.

1979 Traded to the Golden State Warriors.

1980 Begins to miss practices and games as drug addiction takes its toll.

1981 Suspended by Golden State.

1981 Goes to play for the Washington Bullets.

1982 Goes public about his drug use and enters treatment for the first time.

1983 Signs with the San Antonio Spurs.

1984 Signs with the Houston Rockets.

1986 Suspended from the Houston Rockets and enters drug treatment.

1986 Develops a fitness program for people in recovery and succeeds in introducing it to a Houston-area hospital.

1987 Returns to professional basketball to play for the Milwaukee Bucks.

1988 Opens treatment programs for addicted athletes.

1989 Returns to Houston to finish his playing career.

1991 Purchases the Miami Tropics to provide a safe basketball environment for recovering players and coaches.

1992 Becomes head coach of the San Antonio Spurs.

1994 Becomes head coach, general manager, and vice president of basketball operations for the Philadelphia 76ers.

PB   # 1250

PB   # 1250